The Depaı

Introducing a col

T. M. Warren

WRITERS' CHAMPION

T. M. Warren

Copyright © Tyrone M. Warren 2022
Email: trnwrrn@gmail.com

Published by MA Publishing (Penzance)
Website: www.mapublisher.org.uk   Email: mapublisher@yahoo.com
Released on January 2023

Printed in the UK,

ISBN-13: 978-1-910499-98-6

Disclaimer:

All expressions and opinions of the work belong to the artist and MAP and its imprints does not share or endorse any other than to provide the open platform to publish their work. For further information on MAP policies please email: mapublisher@yahoo.com for further information and submission guidelines.

Cover designed by Mayar Akash
Cover image & inside cover page: by Natalie K. Smith (Clacton-on-sea)
Typeset in Times Roman

FSC
www.fsc.org
FSC® C009893

Paper printed on is FSC Certified, lead free, acid free, buffered paper made from wood-based pulp. Our paper meets the ISO 9706 standard for permanent paper. As such, paper will last several hundred years when stored.

2

Dedications

God
My Nana
My Mother
& Hannah

Acknowledgements

MAYAR AKASH
For having the faith in me & gifting me this wonderful opportunity.

ROBERT SMITH
Always being there for me when the consensus thought & voiced otherwise. Opening up the door for me to relocate to Cornwall & being in my presence when I boldly exclaimed to him (last December) that my poetry will be published in the upcoming year.

NATALIE
Blessing me with her beautiful artwork for this book.

TOM VOOGD
For providing me an introduction to my current home as well as his friendship.

TARA MOON
Solid as a rock & never unwavering.

A CHOSEN FEW
That never gave up on me even through the darkest of times
(you know who you are).

CORNWALL
The place where I live & its tranquillity which has benefited me & my writing.

CONTENTS

Dedications	3
Acknowledgements	4
Introduction	7
Stretch Marks	8
Intuition	9
Fire & Air	10
Cuban Smoke	11
The Room Adjacent	12
Uncharted Territories	13
Porridge & Patriarchs	14
3 a.m.	15
The Alchemy of Lovers	16
The Secret	17
The Voyeur	18
The Dance	19
Exhale	20
The Black L7	21
4 Chambers	22
Meena	23
I Am Cumulus	24
The Sweetest Rejection	25
Safe House	26
Bedtime	27
Hunger	28
The Spark	29
The Chord That Binds	30
The Mistress	32
Diagonal	33
Afro Comb	34
The 'Was Was'	35
Maiden Voyage	36
N. F. A.	37
31 Winters	38
Maroon Frequencies	39
Crumlin	40
Blue Globules	41
The Offering	42
Cut Up Experiment (#1)	43
Contraband	44
C.A.S.	45

Cardboard Soul Food	**46**
Past Present Future	**47**
Untitled (#2)	**48**
The Sins of the Father	**49**
The 'Was Was' (#2)	**50**
The Velvet Curtain	**52**
Untitled	**53**
The Sand Is Their Sea	**54**
An Intimate Act	**55**
MAPublisher Catalogue	**57**

Introduction

Tyrone Warren was born in Dublin Ireland to an Irish Mother & West Indian Father & sailed off at the age of 8 to London (England) for a better life.

A Catholic upbringing raised & schooled him until 17 when he left home with a burning curiosity.

Where his time was spent working various jobs & hustles ranging from organising illegal raves, on site graveyard security to running the distribution arm of a well respected independent dance label (Good Looking records).

Falling into addiction & resulting in the inevitable to then pulling a 360' in turning his life around.

"It has been hard work starting from scratch again and I feel gratitude to have had the chance, like God heard my heart. As a way of exploring and connecting with emotions, I looked to writing some poetry. With the encouragement of friends I put it out there and was blessed in having 3 poems published in 'Book of Lived' Vol:8 (Penny Authors)."

Culminating in relocating to Cornwall in early 2021 where he hit the floor running. Tyrone resides at the bottom of a hill, 5 mins from the edge of the Atlantic Ocean, surrounded by the Cornish countryside.

Stretch Marks

I view the state of vulnerability
through the lens of suspicion.

To reveal myself in all
my full-frontal glory.

To cast my line,
the dice have been rolled.
Snake eyes for the warm acknowledgment.

To peer over the edge,
a line crossed over a billion grains of sand.

This vehicle cannot be reversed.
This box now lies open.
4 chambers of the heart exposed
to an atmosphere of judgement.

My cup overflows with my intention,
& leaves a stain on the carpet
that borders between us.

I harbour this vulnerability,
which leaves a blemish on my skin,
like the stretch marks on your hips,
where the shadow of my touch once was,
when we last embraced.

Intuition

Her emotional displays,
bespoke manipulation.
Window dressing
tailored for
the ones who
acknowledged her tactics.
Self-hatred is the
'special guest'
tonight,
with more flaws in her diamond
than a tower block.
As cold as the other side of the pillow,
yet she holds on to me like a ransom.
If loneliness taunts you,
when only your thoughts
lie beside you,
well I don't know what to tell you.
Why engineer
an argument
to hear the
bass in my voice?
Just call me.
This Libran
nature of mine is hindering my focus.
Dysfunctional
romanticism
via a smartphone.
Yet I'm overwhelmed
by my intuition
that burns
caressingly,
like the first fix
thatflushed
my cheeks.

Fire & Air

On a Cornish Summer day,
I long for the touch of a distant flame
I once knew.
To lie together in the tall grass,
greeted by the Summer breeze
on our skin,
like a lover's whisper in one's ear.

Cuban Smoke

The Devil's blue dress
finds residency,
on my bedroom floor.
A once forbidden attraction,
unapologetically free
& devoid of guilt.

2 bloodlines converge.

Base level instincts
collide & screech
to sexual alchemy.
The smell of iron
in the blood.
Metallic climaxes.

The ritual of foreplay
is to be practised
& respected.

My mouth overflows
gathering the dew
of your warm libation,
as I drink at your
fountain.

The spirit of carnality.

The stench of sex
lies heavy in the room,
like billowing clouds
of Cuban smoke,
in the private clubs
of industrialists,
where I'll never gain
entry.

The Room Adjacent

A wall lies between us,
separating the groaning ache
of a desire to embrace another warm body.
We both lie alone in
our individual death poses,
sometimes foetal.

Under the surveillance of the moon.
Can my thoughts penetrate the border between us?
Will she be receptive to the frequency,
& answer the line?
Like a ship in the dark
that catches the lighthouse's eye.

What will she dream of tonight
& am I to be her co-star
in this lonely vignette?

(((Thought forms)))
solidify from the carnal into the sensual.
The unknown is the territory
of our Love.

2 rooms,
2 hearts,
8 chambers.
Both guarded by trust lost,
in the past tense
of a tense past.

Uncharted Territories

Outside my window,
hunched on pylons,
the birds present their evening song as
dusk descends on their tiny
crowns.

Every evening
when sleep takes my hand,
the fog of tiredness
envelops me.

I am the solitary lighthouse
burning the beacon,
shooting my light out
across the murky waters
of the night,
hoping to guide my love
home,
to the safety of my embrace.

Descending into the fog of lucidity,
inviting the darkness
to encase me.
Transporting me off
to uncharted lands.

There is no comparison
to the architecture & territories
that I walk upon.

I will look forward to
tomorrow night,
where I vanish into my dreams
like a teardrop in a rainstorm.

Porridge & Patriarchs

I am looking at my feet,
my small, petite feet,
as a 5-year-old,
eating porridge from the pot,
on the step in the kitchen.

I can hear the voice of Marvin,
making its way down
the corridor
of our 2-bedroom flat.

His voice seems to be
hugging the wall.
Early 80's.

Interrupted
by the radio's announcement.
Then a shriek.
"Marvin Gaye is dead! Shot by his dad!"
I finish my porridge.
Now my Mother is sad.

3 a.m.

The night-time eavesdrops
on my solitude,
& whispers aggressively
at my windowpane.
The shrieks & whirls
are the piper's melody & calling card.
Tap, tap tapping on the glass,
devoid of emotion.
A cold, transparent invasion
into the warmth ofmy sanctuary & sanity.

The Alchemy of Lovers

The blood of 2 strangers.
Drawn together on a grey winter's day
in Dublin's fair City.
Circa 1975.
Resulting in the 3rd.
An alchemical romance.
I am the 3rd.
I am of mixed race.
I am alchemical.
My name is Tyrone!

The Secret

Saw a blind womanthe other day,
walking down the high street in town, with her cain.

Dressed head to toe in black, with shades &
the broadest smile I've ever seen!

"What does she know that the rest of us don't?"

The mirror barks back at our own reflection,
makes you take stock of your own situation.

It is time for gratitude.

The Voyeur

Strangers with contorted faces,
locked in carnal embraces.
I am the voyeur.
The darkness is my cover.
The stage is set.
The pixels vibrate,
the screen is ablaze
but plastic to the touch.
My senses diminished,
my spirit depleted.
What I long for is a human touch,
a warmth,
a breath on my face
to that feverish ache,
that warrants frustration
to the stains I make.
Scenes of needless violence in the night,
not these naked shadows with their
fake light.

The Dance

She awakes the shadow of my carnality,
like a dusty covered light bulb
from yesteryear.

For a split second I see the doubt enter her head,
like a flash in the dark.
I witness her mask slip,
as she presents me
her cleavage.

Summoning a fever,
sparking a memory
of past fornications
& vitality.

I say nothing.
Just reply in silence
with a smile.
We both know the dance &
how it ends.

Exhale

As the flower blooms
her face becomes flushed,
reminiscent of
dusk over ancient Kemet,
when the sand had dominion.

The sensual & carnal
entwine intimately,
relayed through her senses.

Hair is the shade of dark cocoa,
but never as bitter.
Eyes of hazel green
like Medina,
dilated to project desire.

Breathing in trust,
exhaling love.
She feels like warm water, at our most
intimate.

The Black L7

What do you see when you gaze at the black L7?
The End?
The pupil or master?
Depression?
Focus?
Sleep?

Does loneliness reach out to you?

An unplugged T.V screen?
The uncharged smartphone?

Space which inhabits
the blink of an eye?

The purest form of
submission & discipline?

What do you see in the black L7?
Your Queen's next move?
Your own reflection?
Space, without the bright glare
of distractions?
A camera lens?
A Tefelem,
garnished
on the left arm & forehead,
symbolising the
presence of God?

The entrance to a tunnel?

The journey continues.
Where to now?

4 Chambers

The heart wants
what the head can't handle.
A state of emotional undress
towards the feelings addressed.

The heart of the matter.
The bone marrow,
where the flavour's kept.

Entangled wires & currents
remain in the dark,
underneath the respectable sheen of the shell,
while the light remains flickering,
the 4 chambers continue to beat rhythmically
to the sound of her voice,
at the end of the line.

Meena

"The only thing that should be open this late,
is a pair of legs!"
Declared Aunty Meena,
to my 12-year-old self.
It's a Sunday night,
in the mid 80's.

A strong Goan woman
in a 5' 2" frame, with a
mouth like
a car bomb.

A tickle game that bordered on
the inappropriate.
A confidence that oozed
sexuality,
as well as vodka.
Habitually crossing
the line to all newcomers
who tripped her wire,
otherwise known as
'Initiates of the Flame!'

I Am Cumulus

Lying in my bed
circa '83
as an 8-year-old,
location, North London.
Gazing over my bedroom landscape at night.
The door is ajar.
Warm reassurance of the hallway light,
imprints a long golden shard
on the dark plain,
in the plain dark,
I see it all!

My bed is the air,
white cotton sheets encircle me.

I am Cumulus.
I am the cloud.
1 dilated pupil,
in a sea of glacial white,
surveys all that lies below.

I am Cumulus.
8 years of breath is beneath me.
I am the cloud!

The Sweetest Rejection

She swerved my lips
as if I wasn't there,
planting a kiss
on my cheek
& before the sensation
even registered,
she was gone.

Safe House

Our doubts are traitors
who pass on false info.
The dance of manipulation.
Red herrings down dark alleys,
sigils @ dead drops
in familiar places.
Midnight under the
Moon's surveillance.
WE ARE WHAT WE THINK!
Good things come to me easily.
HQ is the subconscious.
The ego is the safe house.
When our paradigm
is challenged,
"Retreat, retreat"!
We shutdown shop.
I repeat:
Stand down!
Burn notice.
Wheels up in 15.
Don't get attached
& never look back.
Fresh face in a new town,
career opportunities.
Today my name is
Mark.

Bedtime

From the cold hand of a stranger under the duvet
that invades the warmth.
To the sound of unfamiliar footsteps
on the stairs.
The foreign scent of the faceless
hangs menacingly in the air.
The inhuman shadow play,
celebrate their dance of death.
Jerking, twisting spasmodically
on a canvas,
illuminated by the
hallway light.
These visions & senses,
the nocturnal motion picture of my early years?
From the over imagination
of this child,
to the penmanship of
this adult.

Hunger

The rain descends on my tin roof,
conjuring the sound
of 1000 impatient fingers,
wrapping in unison on the table.
Rivalled only by the
hunger,
pangs of thunder
echo loudly above me.

The Spark

25 watts of power
via the basement of the subconscious
= desires, emotions & impulses.
INEXHAUSTIBLE!
24/7
365
44 revs
around the Sun God,
the Christos.
I am breath & breath is Life.
Free will,
the spark,
a gift,
the internal maps.
Magnetic North is now South.
Advance no more&
follow your heart!

The Chord That Binds

Is it any surprise
the bed is our
makeshift womb?
Every night when
we feel the cold,
we return to the
foetal position,
which brings warmth.
Memories of
the womb.
One with Mother,
safety, sanctuary.
Creating a
deeply personal relationship,
vanishing
when we inhale
the first breath.
This new world
from the birth canal
into the blinding light.
Life force ripped
from the Mother.
Lungs expel fluid.
A simple snip of silver
& it's over.
We will never be closer
than those 9 months.
You are on your own
now.
Just remain
in the foetal position,
the memory
of a simpler time
shall soon return.
I am cold
&wonder if my

Mother will dream
of me tonight?

The Mistress

Solitude is your lonely mistress
who never backchats,
doesn't second guess,
nor does she challenge you.
She is your blanket, your roaring fire,
the city skyline through the window of your sanctuary.

Outside & its inhabitants are frowned upon.
Disliked, mocked & mistrusted.
She will always be the longest,
strongest relationship you've had.

Solitude is your mistress,
you've always known this
hence why you'll never show her the door.

Diagonal

They go backwards,
we go forwards.
It gets deeper & deeper.
They go forwards,
we go backwards.
It gets deeper & deeper.

Memories in the
modern day.

Am I going backwards
while they go forward?
Na, dead that!
I'm going sideways.
Diagonal.
Not backwards,
never under.

Forget the absence.
Forgive the Father.

Mock rejection.
Roll the dice
&play the numbers.
Embrace the present.
Go all out,
act the fool,
make the jump,
reveal too much,
get clingy,
feel hurt,
get out,
press pause,
take stock,
breathe in,
exhale!

Afro Comb

The strength is in your hair,
like the Lion's mane
& Samson curls.

Militant locks, caressed by
beeswax
to a roots, rock riddim!

Hair like lamb's wool (pre-B.C)
to D.C (chocolate city).
"We got tha funk!"

Skin tone resembling copper
from the time of the Pharaohs
to future coups,
where the sugarcane & coco leaf grow.

From the 12 tribes
my blood runs back to Benjamin.
Mahogany royalty.
Penthouse to pavement.

Your hair does not define you,
it is a statement.
Lay down your arms,
pick up ya comb!

The 'Was Was'

Do you hear them?
Do you hear their whispers?
Do you hear the sound of the
'Was Was'
on the back of your neck?
Feel their secrets?

Do you hear them?
Can you hear the sounds,
of their whispers,
their darkinsights?
Can you hear them?
The'Was Was'
near your ear?

Maiden Voyage

Let me return to the water's embrace.
Recollections of deliverance & wonder.

Creation through the scream
of the Mother.

As the dam breaks,
the baby crowns.
A new King is born.

The chord severed, yet the bond
remains unbroken.

First light invades the
Darkness.
To exit the tunnel,
the soul is illuminated.

This vessel has been birthed,
its maiden voyage awaits.

N. F. A.

Like a helpless romantic
trying to French kiss a brass,
I am lonely.

Lonely does
what loneliness sees.

The distance between 2 spaces
erupts an emotion,
the tear ducts empty
&cheeks become stained.
Moisture born
from joy & pain.

I fly the flag of a coward
when it comes to affairs of the heart.
I'd rather hang out of you
than hang out with you.
A connection through a feeling
that never starts.

Emotional availability
left the building years ago.
This room is bare,
the lights are off,
the lock is broken.
No one's home.
You've come to the
wrong place.

31 Winters

Emotional disturbances
& investigative reports.

My nature shines brightly
on your dimly lit street,
which leads me to the epiphany:
For 31 winters I've been trying
to make my way
back home.

Spoken in the vernacular
of silence.

The window is broken,
yet the way the rain
leaves its stain
on the glass,
reminds me of yesterday's
heartbreaks
& tomorrow's betrayals.

Maroon Frequencies

The spirit of jealousy looms
heavily in my thoughts today.
The cold hiss of its dialect invades my ear
& the acidic stench smothers my pallet.

A familiar entity returns to mock me.
Sadness & self-doubt
envelope me like
the scales of a sitar,
to the pit of my stomach.

Dark silhouettes jerk & slither
on white bed sheets.
The voyeur is now in the building.
My mind permeated
with the sensation of a desire
not realised.

Can this summit be reached?
Maroon frequencies illuminate
rudimentary possibilities.

Guide me safely to the warm
waters of your reassurance,
bypassing the personality defects
from yesteryear.

This moral compass that we all
adhere to, has been inverted
for decades.

We are all just that solitary pedestrian,
walking along the motorway
@ midnight,
with the oncoming traffic
at our backs.

Crumlin

When I think of home
I find myself transported
back to Dublin's permanent
grey skies &
cobbled streets.
Landsdowne Rd.
The smell of coal,
burning wood
invades, caressing
my nostrils.
Aromatic storytelling.
The feeling of belonging
& fellowship.
Grey clouds relieving themselves.
Windows shedding teardrops,
as the storm clouds gather
in a scrum over Crumlin.
I reminisce about playing curbies
with a cheap football, bought
only for the wind to hijack it
& lead it astray.
Boiled tripe wafts out of
Nanas kitchen,
while the ice cream van
sounds the alarm,
setting off a Pavlovian instinct.
Parents dig in their
pockets for silver shrapnel.
99's & the latest video nasties to rent.
The rain, the wind.
Family = security.
Happiness can be just a
mere sentence or a paragraph.
It's the words we choose
to accommodate that space,
that means everything.

Blue Globules

Mirror meditation,
reflecting a stranger
towards the eyes of the familiar.
They assume I have the spark
but I only have the kindling.
Drawing symbols
to excavate
subconscious theories.
Mentally processing my
way out of existence.
I need nature
by my side,
like a brass needs a trick.
Calmness soothes me,
like old bus routes
& folding tissues.
Looking up to
the sea of blue,
unblemished
by skylines,
the Sun God,
casts his gaze down at me.
70's neon tangerine,
bogey green &
electric blue globules
dance on the black
backdrop of my
eyelids,
whenever I'm in
his presence.

The Offering

Someone's blood will be
signing the pavement tonight,
because ecstasy
is found somewhere
between
the screech
& the impact of
colliding metal.
The crows, as 1, eclipse
the sky,
honouring the ritual of
deaths descent.
These fevered dreams
consume him
as offerings & tribunes
to Hecate
at the High table.

Cut Up Experiment (#1)

Entertainment over enlightenment,
the poison pocket of your subconscious.
The vexation of my spirit.
The inner child who is comfortable in his own skin,
who overcame the demons
within.
The communal room, where
everyone perceives the same dream.
Nicotine copper-stained fingertips point, accusingly.
The cheap fragrance called jealousy worn by little girls & boys.
The tender mercies.
{Whispers} "I see you. Hold my hand & never fear the dark!"
I am not your project, nor your canvas to project
your insecurities onto.
A guide for the perplexed.
"Hell is empty & all the devils are here"
as William once wrote!
Worldly winds.

(I used William Burroughs 'cut up' technique. Putting 13 small pieces of paper, with ideas for poems on, in a pot, I then closed my eyes &picked them out 1 by 1. They were laid out in a grid &as I opened each one, I read out loud. The above is the result. I used the same technique to decide the order the poems would appear in the book).

Contraband

We are contraband.
We live in suitcases,
crevices.
We are to be secreted.
We are invisible,
quiet.
We cross borders.
Physical,
mental,
behavioural.
To dwell in the darkness.
Goosebumps raised.
Contraband.
We exist to execute.
Running down the skin
of free will,
on the individual.
We are contraband.
Warm liquid
running down skin.
Goosebumps raised.
Memories of a gashed head,
to be taken by the hand,
led astray.
Warm liquid.
To be spellbound.
Goosebumps raised.
Advance no more
&retreat into the
embrace of distraction.

C.A.S.

Suede fingertips & silk palms
surf across my chest, caressing
my flesh,
as if it were ancient braille on a Persian artefact,
smuggled down through
bloodlines.
Hairs stand erect,
to attention, like magnetised
metal filings in a Roman formation.
She visits me between 4-5am,
in the form of deep crimson smoke.
At the point where
you're unaware
of the sound of your own
breath & heartbeat.
To the debutant, her form may look blurry to the eye,
yet at a 2nd glance,
looks dense.
Intricate, revealing an infinity
of curves
among curls
among curves
among curls.
To gaze among this, is to instantly feel
with every eye-blink.
She communicates to me via my nerve endings,
in a dialect of comfort
arousal & sensuality.
Erogenous zones, left for certain pronunciation,
with force applied.
Nose bleeds have been known to occur, as the pressure
in the room changes,
causing my ears to pop, which often
signals her imminent arrival.
To deny these experiences is like trying to hold back the tides of the
Oceans.

Cardboard Soul Food

I am one of many,
at the banquet hall of hungry ghosts.

Gluttonous,
the nonstop feast
that fails to satisfy & nourish
one's own appetite,
& quench the thirst of my parched
soul & sanity!

Past Present Future

With the sonic charge of 1000 pipers saluting the chieftain,
I become enhanced by the music of the Black Watch.
Mahogany bloodlines.

They revel in their decibels of destruction.
My creation rises silently,
taking flight.
Alchemical.

Every night I take to my bed, amongst the machines of untapped
possibilities.

Is it only when I awaken, they sing their siren song?

We are the present,
created in the past,
yet our dreams are basedin the future.

Unforeseen entities
manifest into matter,
otherwise known
as spirits
to the uninformed.

While foreign installations lic festering in my psyche,
once revealed by Castaneda, many moons ago.

It's like looking at
old photographs of yesteryear,
without a dry eye.

Untitled (#2)

Uncontrollable 4 dimensional
thinking = Dreams.
Transmutation of the soul
in the dead of night.
Surrender to the mattress.
Storytelling to express one's emotions during the waking hour.
Early childhood development to
advance the psyche
is a must.
Beware those tendrils of guilt
that slither around your frame,
like vines embracing the sun.
Searching for the Matriarch's
blessing,
to validate the son's existence.
All things in the fire burn.
All things shall pass.

The Sins of the Father

Am I destined to make the mistake,
of returning to the place, where I pull the blanket over my head?

To press pause on my life, to shutdown yet again?

Auxiliary power.

Brought here by rejection,
9 letters that cut deep.

The sins of the Father via Patriarchal absences,
live on, through modern day romantic rejection.

An open wound that can't be stitched.

Memories of days passed bubble up
to the surface,
grinning with faces like mirrors, reflecting my tears & the fears of
self-doubt,
which I thought I'd laid to rest in
Davy Jones's locker.

Now my bed lies empty once again,
awaiting the warmth of my
sorrow & solitude.

The 'Was Was' (#2)

Whisperings & insights from
the 'Was Was,'
return to me.
The stench of their
fetid breath,
fondle the base
of my neck.
Self-doubt reawakens
from its slumber,
presenting itself
from behind the mask
of my reflection,
gaining entrance into
the fortress of
my confidence.

No gods.
No monsters.
Just the 'Was Was.

Self-hatred personified,
nurtured from
a polluted womb of
blood,
shit,
& cum.
Delivered into the
light,
from the birth canal
of misery.

Tongues that tingle
reveal glances of your origin.
Hairs raised on clammy
grey skin,
born out of an assault,

raised on abuse.
Genuine affection,
connections,
speed past my station,
onward bound,
towards another
man's arms.

No gods.
No monsters.

You are damaged goods
on a dusty shelf
of optimism,
with a sad story to tell
& good hair!

The 'Was Was'
who whisper
their insights,
hissing
their offerings,
penetrating my eardrums.
Now can you hear them?

Do you hear the sound
of the 'Was Was?'

The Velvet Curtain

The clarity of the Cornish night sky reminds me:
Space
is a mass of crushed black velvet,
speckled with pin pricks
made by God's own finger.
What we mortals comprehend
as stars,
are just the pure light of heaven,
bursting through the cracks
of the black curtain bordering
our 2 worlds.
Shine on!

Untitled

Windows rattle in unison,
delivering a future echo, signifying chaos's imminent arrival.
Outside is the playground for
mischief & destruction.
No borders respected.
No places of worship overlooked.
This force,
this original tenant,
was here aeons before,
& will continue to roam, long time after witnessing our fates pass by.
Nature has left the building
& is now in my backyard!
Has the wind been eavesdropping on my road to self-improvement?
Gaining a deeper understanding of who I am
& what I can be?
Has the wind been pressing against my windows all this time?
Collecting, compiling
a file on me,
disguised under the soundtrack of whirls & shrieks?
Listening…
Listening…
What stake has nature in my transformation of self?
The clarity of revelation dawns on me:
The last pangs of self-doubt &
hatred, cocooned
around me for decades, have been exorcised.
Banished from my mind & soul,
channelled into the form of a storm
outside my window.
Alchemy.
Metamorphosis.
As the skin sheds the past,
a new outlook for the future
emerges.

The Sand Is Their Sea

Enchanted by aromas of yesteryear,
where the sand has dominion,
transported on the breeze via the cumulus.

A fantastic voyage.
Saffron, paprika, cumin.
Magnetic North, towards the red city
in which I dwell.

I inhale inspiration from a far-off place.
Where the sand consumes the city.
Where the dialect of an
ancient feline bloodline
'Mahogany Royalty' was taught to me.
The subtle mannerisms of an eye blink,
to control &
translate what is being conveyed.
Never to reveal their secrets.

An Intimate Act

I am a man who's been stranded at sea for far too long.
The coconut oil is the vessel.
My desire is the wind that propels it forward.

Her olive skin is the undiscovered continent
that awaits my arrival
& exploration.
2 green eyes stare out at me,
like burning beacons, guiding me
to safety.

So far from home,
yet so familiar.

My hands need no compass as I've been here before,
"The map is not the territory!" as Mr Wilson
once exclaimed.

A déjà vu
revealed through an intimate act,
an erotic sensation.

If I was with her now
I would remove this emotional mask
& cast away this armour of self-doubt,
that has been tailored to hide my
insecurities & imperfections.

To stand there naked before her.
Garnished in my
regret,
blemishes & scars
of failure,
without breaking eye contact.

Alone again, once more on the Ocean,

all I am left with,
to accompany her memory,
is her smell,
which I cherish to this day.

MAPublisher Catalogue

ISBN/Titles /Image/Author	ISBN/Titles /Image/Author	ISBN/Titles /Image/Author	ISBN/Titles /Image/Author
978-1-910499-00-9 Father to child By Mayar Akash	978-1-910499-08-5 HSJ Lakri Tura By Mayar Akash	978-1-910499-26-9 Colouring 1-10 By MAPublisher	978-1-910499-18-4 Basic Numbers 1-10 By MAPublisher
978-1-910499-16-0 River of Life By Mayar Akash	978-1-910499-09-2 HSJ Gilaf Procession By Mayar Akash	978-1-910499-27-6 Activity Numbers 1-10 By MAPublisher	978-1-910499-19-1 Number 1-100 By MAPublisher
978-1-910499-39-9 Eyewithin By Mayar Akash	978-1-910499-03-0 HSJ Mazar Sharif By Mayar Akash	978-1-910499-28-3 Activity Colouring Alphabets By MAPublisher	978-1-910499-20-7 Vowels By MAPublisher
978-1-910499-32-0 WG Survivor By Mayar Akash	978-1-910499-06-1 Hazrat Shahjalal By Mayar Akash	978-1-910499-68-9 The Adventures of Sylheti mazars By Mayar Akash	978-1-910499-21-4 Alphabet Consonants By MAPublisher
978-1-910499-66-5 Yesteryears By Mayar Akash	978-1-910499-07-8 HSJ Urus By Mayar Akash	978-1-910499-38-2 Bite Size Islam: 99 Names of Allah By Mayar Akash	978 1-910499-22-1 Vowels & Short By MAPublisher

ISBN/Titles /Image/Author	ISBN/Titles /Image/Author	ISBN/Titles /Image/Author	ISBN/Titles /Image/Author
978-1-910499-15-3 Anthology One By Penny Authors	978-1-910499-36-8 Delirious By Liam Newton	978-1-910499-52-8 Lit From Within By Ruth Lewarne	978-1-910499-57-3 The Vampire of the Resistance By Ruth Lewarne
978-1-910499-17-7 Anthology Two By Penny Authors	978-1-910499-54-2 Book of Lived v6 Penny Authors	978-1-910499-49-8 Cry for Help By B. M. Gandhi	978-1-910499-55-9 Riversolde By Meriyon
978-1-910499-29-0 Book of Lived v3 By Penny Authors	978-1-910499-37-5 When You Look Back By Rashma Mehta	978-1-910499-14-6 The Halloweeen Poem by Zainab Khan	978-1-910499-70-2 Smiley & The Acorn By Roger Underwood
978-1-910499-351 V4 Book of Lived By Penny Authors	978-1-910499-37-5 My Dream World By Rashma Mehta	978-1-910499-69-6 Consciousness By Mustak Mustafa	978-1-910499-40-5 World's First University By Giasuddin Ahmed
978-1-910499-50-4 Book of Lived v5 By Penny Authors	978-1-910499-53-5 Angel Eyez By Rashma Mehta	978-1-910499-73-3 Book of Lived v7 By Penny Authors	978-1-910499-56-6 The Warrior Queen By Giasuddin Ahmed

www.mapublisher.org.uk

ISBN/Titles /Image/Author	ISBN/Titles /Image/Author	ISBN/Titles /Image/Author	ISBN/Titles /Image/Author
978-1-910499-58-0 Tower Hamlets, Random, One Mayar Akash	978-1-910499-60-3 Tower Hamlets, Random, Two By Mayar Akash	978-1-910499-05-4 Tide of Change By Mayar Akash	978-1-910499-51-1 Brick & Mortar By Mayar Akash
978-1-910499-61-0 Grenfell Tower By Mayar Akash	978-1-910499-63-4 Power Houses By Mayar Akash	978-1-910499-71-9 Altab Ali Murder By Mayar Akash	978-1-910499-31-3 Pathfinders By Mayar Akash
978-1-910499-62-7 Community Service 1992-1993 By Mayar Akash	978-1-910499-64-1 Bancroft Estate By Mayar Akash	978-1-910499-11-5 Re-Awakening By Mayar Akash	978-1-910499-13-9 Chronicle of Sylhetis of UK By Mayar Akash
978-1-910499-59-7 Brick Lane, Spitalfields By Mayar Akash	978-1-910499-72-6 25th Anniversary of Bangladesh By Mayar Akash	978-1-910499-12-2 Young Voice Mayar Akash	978-1-910499-42-9 Bangladeshi Fishes By Mayar Akash
978-1-910499-65-8 PYO Polish Exchange 1992 By Mayar Akash	978-1-910499-30-6 TH Bangladeshi Politicians By Mayar Akash	978-1-910499-10-8 Vigil Subotaged By Mayar Akash	978-1-910499-67-2 F. Ahmed and History By Mukid Choudhury

www.mapublisher.org.uk

ISBN/Titles /Image/Author	ISBN/Titles /Image/Author	ISBN/Titles /Image/Author	ISBN/Titles /Image/Author
978-1-910499-43-6 My Life Book 1 By Mayar Akash	978-1-910499-44-3 My Life Book 2 By Mayar Akash	978-1-910499-45-0 My Life Book 3 By Mayar Akash	978-1-910499-46-7 My Life Book 4 By Mayar Akash
978-1-910499-47-4 My Life Book 5 By Mayar Akash	978-1-910499-75-7 Bangladeshis in Manchester - Oral History, Part 1 By M.A. Mustak	978-1-910499-74-0 Peter Fox Artist (LE) A Re-enchantment of Contemporary Art By Peter Fox	978-1-910499-78-8 On The Seventh Day By Cosette Ratliff
978-1-910499-79-5 Altab Ali Life & Family By Mayar Akash	978-1-910499-77-1 Smiley & the Acorn Treasure on the Isles of Scilly By Roger Underwood	978-1-910499-80-1 India – stories from the Banyan Tree Paul Wadsworth	978-1-910499-84-9 V8 Book of lived Penny Authors
978-1-910499-87-0 Behind the tears Rashma Mehta	978-1-910499-85-6 RhythmScripts My Feet is just mine Libby Pentreath	978-1-910499-89-4 Podgy and the Delightful Company John Dillon	978-1-910499-90-0 Calm and the Storm Alison Norton
978-1-910499-88-7 Pebble Libby Pentreath	978-1-910499-91-7 The Crab's Tale John Dillon	978-1-910499-92-4 Res Burman's Poetry V1 Res J. F. Burman	978-1-910499-93-1 Res Burman's Poetry v2 Res J. F. Burman

www.mapublisher.org.uk

ISBN/Titles /Image/Author	ISBN/Titles /Image/Author	ISBN/Titles /Image/Author	ISBN/Titles /Image/Author
978-1-910499-96-2 Lowry's Boats Roger Lowry	978-1-910499-97-9 Who is? Tilesky Mayar Akash	978-1-910499-23-8 Altab Ali The Symbol Mayar Akash	978-1-910499-24-5 Montol Mayar Akash

www.mapublisher.org.uk

Printed and bound by CPI Group (UK) Ltd, Croydon, CR0 4YY

20/10/2024

01776483-0009